GUIDE DOGS FOR THE BLIND

Training, Care, and Stories

By

Elliot Rivers

Copyright Notice

Disclaimer

The information provided in this book is intended for general informational purposes only. While every effort has been made to ensure the accuracy and reliability of the content, the author and publisher do not accept any responsibility for errors, omissions, or any outcomes that may arise from the use of the information contained herein.

The book does not substitute professional advice, and readers should seek the advice of qualified professionals, particularly in areas related to guide dog training, animal care, health, and safety.

References to specific organizations, products, or services are not endorsements, nor are they intended to imply any form of partnership, association, or sponsorship unless explicitly stated.

The author and publisher also reserve the right to update or modify any information provided in the book at their discretion.

CONTENT

Chapter Eight

Chapter Nine

Chapter Ten

CHAPTER ONE

The History and Evolution of

Guide Dogs

Ancient Beginnings: The Earliest Bonds

The relationship between humans and dogs dates back thousands of years, with evidence suggesting that dogs have assisted humans in various capacities since ancient times. One of the earliest known depictions of a guide dog helping a blind person is a first-century AD mural discovered in the ruins of Roman Herculaneum. This artwork illustrates a dog leading a blind man, indicating that the concept of guide dogs has ancient origins.

The First World War: A Catalyst for Change

The modern guide dog movement began during World War I, a period that saw a significant number of soldiers returning home with visual impairments due to injuries sustained in combat. Recognizing the need for support, Dr. Gerhard Stalling in Germany initiated a program to train dogs to assist these individuals. In 1916, he established the world's first guide dog school for the blind in Oldenburg, Germany. The school trained up to 600 dogs annually, assisting not only German veterans but also blind individuals in other countries, including Britain, France, and the United States.

The Seeing Eye: Pioneering Guide Dog Training in the U.S.

In 1927, American dog trainer Dorothy Harrison Eustis wrote an article about the German guide dog programs, which inspired Morris Frank, a young blind man from Tennessee. Eustis agreed to train Frank in Switzerland, and 1928, he returned to the United States with his guide dog, Buddy. Demonstrating the effectiveness of guide dogs, Frank and Buddy navigated the busy streets of New York City, capturing public attention. This success led to the founding of The Seeing Eye in 1929, the first guide dog school in the United States, which has since matched over 17,500 guide dog teams.

The United Kingdom: Establishing Guide Dogs for the Blind

Inspired by developments abroad, the United Kingdom saw the formation of its own guide dog program in 1931, initiated by Muriel Crooke and Rosamund Bond. They trained the first British guide dogs—Judy, Flash, Folly, and Meta—in a garage in Wallasey, Merseyside. Despite initial skepticism, the program gained acceptance, leading to the establishment of the Guide Dogs for the Blind Association in 1934. Over the years, the organization has transformed thousands of lives through guide dog partnerships.

Global Expansion: Guide Dogs Around the World

The success of guide dog programs in the U.S. and the U.K. inspired similar initiatives worldwide. In Australia, Dr. Arnold Cook introduced the first guide dog, Dreana, in 1950 after training in England. This led to the establishment of Guide Dogs Australia, which now operates across the country, providing essential services to individuals with vision impairments.

Advancements in Breeding and Training

Modern guide dog programs have embraced scientific advancements to enhance breeding and training processes. For instance, the UK charity Guide Dogs employs comprehensive genetic data and behavioral assessments to select optimal breeding pairs. A notable example is Terry, a Labrador-Golden Retriever crossbred for ideal traits such as confidence and adaptability. These advancements aim to produce dogs best suited for guide work, ensuring successful partnerships.

Celebrating the Human-Canine Bond

The profound bond between guide dogs and their handlers is exemplified in numerous real-life stories. One notable account is that of Michael Hingson and his guide dog, Roselle. On September 11, 2001, Roselle led Hingson down 78 flights of stairs to safety from the World Trade Center. Their story is detailed in the best-selling book Thunder Dog: The True Story of a Blind Man, His Guide Dog, and the Triumph of Trust at Ground Zero.

CHAPTER TWO

Understanding Visual Impairments

and Mobility Needs

1. Introduction to Visual Impairments

Visual impairment encompasses a range of conditions that affect an individual's ability to see. These impairments can be congenital or acquired and vary in severity. Understanding the spectrum of visual impairments is crucial for appreciating the challenges faced by those affected and the role guide dogs play in mitigating these challenges.

Types of Visual Impairments

Low Vision: This refers to a significant visual impairment that cannot be fully corrected with glasses, contact lenses, medication, or surgery. Individuals with low vision may have blurred vision, blind spots, or tunnel vision.

Blindness: This term is used when a person has no vision or only light perception. It can be congenital or result from conditions such as glaucoma, macular degeneration, or diabetic retinopathy.

Cortical Visual Impairment (CVI): CVI is caused by damage to the visual pathways or visual processing centers in the brain, rather than the eyes themselves. It is now recognized as a leading cause of visual impairment in children.

2. Impact on Daily Life and Mobility

Visual impairments significantly affect an individual's ability to navigate their environment safely and independently. Challenges include:

- **Orientation Difficulties:** Understanding one's position in space and relation to other objects becomes challenging, leading to disorientation.

- **Obstacle Avoidance:** Detecting and avoiding obstacles, especially those at head level or protruding objects, is difficult.

- Route Planning: Planning and following a route, especially in unfamiliar environments, poses a significant challenge.

- **Public Transportation:** Using buses, trains, or subways requires the ability to read signs, schedules, and navigate complex stations.

3. Traditional Mobility Aids

Before the widespread use of guide dogs, individuals with visual impairments relied on various tools to aid mobility:

- **White Cane:** A widely recognized symbol of blindness, the white cane helps detect obstacles and changes in surface textures. It also signals to others that the user has a visual impairment.

- **Human Guide:** Relying on another person for assistance in navigation, especially in unfamiliar or crowded environments.

- **Electronic Aids:** Devices such as sonar-based tools or GPS systems provide auditory or tactile feedback to assist in navigation.

4. The Role of Guide Dogs

Guide dogs offer a unique combination of mobility assistance and companionship. Their training enables them to:

- **Navigate Obstacles:** Guide dogs are trained to avoid obstacles, stop at curbs and stairs, and navigate around hazards.

- **Provide Direction:** While the handler provides commands, the guide dog assists in maintaining a straight path and making turns.

- **Ensure Safety**: Guide dogs are trained in "intelligent disobedience," meaning they will disobey a command if it would lead the handler into danger, such as moving into traffic.

- **Enhance Confidence:** The presence of a guide dog often increases the handler's confidence, encouraging more independent travel and social interaction.

5. Matching Guide Dogs with Handlers

The process of pairing a guide dog with a handler is meticulous:

- **Assessment:** Organizations assess the individual's lifestyle, mobility needs, and personality to ensure a suitable match.

- **Training:** Once matched, the handler undergoes training to learn how to work effectively with the guide dog, establishing communication and trust.

- **Ongoing Support:** Many organizations provide continued support, including follow-up visits and refresher training sessions.

6. Benefits Beyond Mobility

Beyond aiding in navigation, guide dogs offer additional benefits:

- **Emotional Support:** The companionship of a guide dog can alleviate feelings of isolation and depression.

- **Social Interaction:** Guide dogs often serve as social bridges, facilitating conversations and interactions that might not occur otherwise.

- **Physical Health:** Handlers often experience increased physical activity levels, contributing to overall health and well-being.

7. Challenges and Considerations

While guide dogs offer numerous benefits, there are considerations to keep in mind:

- **Care and Maintenance:** Owning a guide dog requires a commitment to the dog's health, including regular veterinary care, grooming, and exercise.

- **Public Access:** Despite laws protecting the rights of guide dog handlers, individuals may still face challenges accessing certain public spaces.

- **Compatibility:** Not all individuals with visual impairments are suitable candidates for guide dog ownership due to factors like lifestyle, allergies, or inability to care for the dog.

Conclusion

Understanding the spectrum of visual impairments and their impact on mobility underscores the invaluable role guide dogs play in enhancing independence and quality of life. As we continue to explore the world of guide dogs, it becomes evident that these animals are not just tools for navigation but partners in life's journey.

CHAPTER THREE

Breeds Best Suited for Guide

Dog Work

Introduction

Choosing the right breed for guide dog work is one of the most critical aspects of the guide dog training process. Guide dogs must be intelligent, trainable, and have a temperament that is well-suited for the high demands of guiding people with visual impairments. While training techniques and care are crucial, the breed itself lays the foundation for success. Certain breeds consistently perform well in guide dog programs due to their innate qualities—intelligence, focus, adaptability, and calmness. This chapter delves into the best breeds for guide dog work, why these breeds excel, and how their specific traits make them particularly well-suited for the role of assisting individuals with visual impairments.

In this chapter, we will focus on the most common and effective breeds used in guide dog programs, including Labrador Retrievers, Golden Retrievers, German Shepherds, Poodles, and other breeds that have shown promise in specific contexts. We will explore their characteristics, temperament, and the factors that make them ideal for the job. We will also look at the genetic and behavioral traits that contribute to their success as guide dogs and how these traits influence breed selection.

1. Labrador Retrievers: The Undisputed Leader

Labrador Retrievers are by far the most commonly used breed for guide dog work worldwide. Their popularity in guide dog programs can be attributed to their exceptional combination of intelligence, work ethic, and friendly, non-aggressive nature. The Labrador's natural eagerness to please its handler, coupled with its high intelligence, makes them incredibly easy to train. These dogs are known for their cooperative nature, which is essential for the close bond required between guide dog and handler.

Key Traits:

- **Intelligence:** Labradors are highly intelligent and can learn tasks quickly. This trait is essential for guide dog training, where dogs must learn to perform complex tasks and navigate busy, unpredictable environments.

- **Temperament:** Labradors are known for their friendly, calm, and patient temperament. They are less likely to be aggressive or easily stressed, which makes them ideal for working with individuals who may have anxiety or stress-related issues.

- **Adaptability:** Labs can adapt to various environments, from busy urban streets to quieter rural areas. Their ability to adjust to new settings and situations makes them versatile in guide dog roles.

- **Size:** Labradors are medium-sized dogs, making them easy to handle and suitable for individuals of varying physical abilities.

Labradors are particularly effective in guide dog work because of their natural ability to guide and their willingness to perform. They thrive in structured environments where they can be given clear tasks and roles. Their joyful demeanor and eagerness to please their handlers make them the go-to breed for guide dog programs.

2. Golden Retrievers: The Gentle Companion

Golden Retrievers are another popular breed in guide dog programs. Known for their gentle nature and strong bond with humans, Golden Retrievers excel in environments where a calm and patient demeanor is crucial. Their affectionate personality and intelligence make them ideal companions for individuals with visual impairments.

Key Traits:

- **Intelligence:** Like the Labrador, Golden Retrievers are highly intelligent and quick learners. Their intelligence allows them to master the complex tasks required for guide dog work, including navigating obstacles, understanding commands, and adjusting to their handler's needs.

- **Temperament:** Golden Retrievers are known for their gentle, friendly nature. They are extremely patient and compassionate, making them great companions for individuals with disabilities. Their calm temperament helps them remain composed even in high-stress environments.

- **Social Sensitivity:** Golden Retrievers are naturally attuned to human emotions and needs, which makes them particularly adept at working with people who rely on them for guidance and support.

- **Trainability:** Golden Retrievers are easy to train, responding well to positive reinforcement techniques. Their strong desire to please their handlers makes them highly trainable, which is essential for guide dog work.

Golden Retrievers are particularly suited for individuals who need a guide dog with a calm and nurturing demeanor. Their ability to adapt to different environments and their strong bond with their handlers make them one of the most trusted breeds in guide dog programs.

3. Labrador-Golden Retriever Crosses: The Best of Both Worlds

While both Labrador Retrievers and Golden Retrievers excel individually in guide dog work, many programs have started using crosses between the two breeds to combine the best traits of both. Labrador-Golden Retriever crosses are known for their balanced temperament, intelligence, and adaptability. This crossbreed benefits from the Labrador's strong work ethic and the Golden's gentle nature, creating a guide dog with the best qualities of both breeds.

Key Traits:

- **Hybrid Vigor:** Crossbreeding often results in "hybrid vigor," where the offspring inherit the best characteristics from both parent breeds. This can lead to healthier dogs with fewer genetic issues and more stable temperaments.

- **Balanced Temperament:** The Labrador-Golden Retriever cross tends to have a very balanced temperament—energetic yet calm, intelligent yet patient. These dogs are highly adaptable and can excel in a variety of environments.

- **Trainability and Intelligence:** As with both parent breeds, Labrador-Golden Retriever crosses are highly trainable and eager to please. They learn quickly and enjoy the training process, which is essential for guide dog work.

This crossbreed is especially effective for guide dog programs because of its well-rounded nature. These dogs can work in both busy urban environments and quieter rural areas, and they can be matched with clients who have varying needs.

4. German Shepherds: Loyalty and Intelligence

German Shepherds were one of the first breeds used as guide dogs, and while they are less common today in guide dog programs, they still have a strong presence. Known for their loyalty, intelligence, and work ethic, German Shepherds excel in tasks that require precision and problem-solving. However, their strong protective instincts and sensitivity to environmental stressors make them more suited to specific guide dog roles.

Key Traits:

- **Intelligence:** German Shepherds are highly intelligent dogs that excel at learning complex tasks. They are often used in police and military work because of their ability to think critically and solve problems.

- **Loyalty:** German Shepherds are known for their deep loyalty to their handlers. This bond is important in guide dog work, where a strong connection between the dog and handler is essential for success.

- **Protectiveness:** While their protective instincts can be a positive trait in some contexts, they can also be a challenge when working as a guide dog. Some German Shepherds may be overly cautious or reactive to unfamiliar people or situations.

- **Strength:** German Shepherds are strong dogs that can assist handlers in physically demanding situations, such as navigating difficult terrain or carrying out complex tasks.

German Shepherds are still used in guide dog programs, but they are often paired with handlers who need a more assertive and protective companion. They excel in environments that require their strong work ethic and loyalty, but they may not be the best fit for every handler.

5. Poodles: The Hypoallergenic Option

Poodles, particularly Standard Poodles, are gaining popularity in guide dog programs, especially for individuals with allergies. Poodles are known for their intelligence, agility, and hypoallergenic coats, which make them a good option for people who may be sensitive to dog dander. While not as commonly used as Labradors or Golden Retrievers, Poodles have shown themselves to be highly effective in guide dog roles.

Key Traits:

- **Intelligence:** Poodles are one of the smartest dog breeds. They excel at learning commands and tasks quickly, which makes them ideal for guide dog training.

- **Hypoallergenic Coat:** Poodles have a unique, curly coat that produces less dander than most other breeds, making them a good choice for individuals with allergies.

- **Trainability:** Poodles are highly trainable, responding well to structured training techniques. Their natural agility and responsiveness make them great guide dogs, particularly for handlers who need a smaller, hypoallergenic dog.

- **Agility:** Poodles are known for their agility, making them excellent at navigating challenging environments.

While their grooming needs are higher than those of other breeds, Poodles are well-suited for individuals who need a hypoallergenic guide dog that is intelligent, agile, and easy to train.

6. Other Breeds and Considerations

While the aforementioned breeds are the most commonly used in guide dog programs, several other breeds have also shown promise in specific circumstances. Breeds like Boxers, Flat-Coated Retrievers, and Smooth Collies have been successfully trained as guide dogs in various parts of the world.

Key Considerations:

- **Boxers:** Known for their playful and affectionate nature, Boxers are sometimes used as guide dogs in programs where a more energetic and lively companion is needed.

- **Flat-Coated Retrievers:** These dogs share many characteristics with Golden Retrievers, including their friendly disposition and trainability. They are often used in guide dog programs where a larger dog is required.

- **Smooth Collies:** Smooth Collies are sometimes used for guide work due to their calm temperament and excellent trainability. They are particularly effective for clients in more rural or suburban settings.

The choice of breed can also depend on the specific needs of the handler. Some individuals may require a smaller dog for ease of handling in crowded urban environments, while others may need a larger dog for assistance with mobility.

7. Breed Suitability and Client Matching

Matching the right dog to the right client is an essential part of guide dog programs. Factors such as the client's mobility needs, walking pace, environment, and personality must be considered when selecting a guide dog. The breed of the dog plays a significant role in this matching process, as certain breeds are better suited for particular tasks or environments.

For example, a Golden Retriever or Labrador may be ideal for someone living in a busy city, as these dogs are calm and adaptable in crowded areas. Conversely, a German Shepherd may be better suited to a client who requires a more assertive dog in outdoor or less structured environments.

8. Health and Longevity Considerations

Health is a primary concern in the selection of guide dog breeds. Guide dogs must be physically fit, free from hereditary conditions, and able to serve their handler for many years. Health considerations include screening for conditions like hip dysplasia, cataracts, and other breed-specific disorders.

Breed programs carefully monitor the health of their breeding stock, ensuring that only dogs with excellent health records are selected for breeding. This helps reduce the risk of passing on hereditary health issues to future generations of guide dogs.

9. The Role of Individual Temperament

While breed traits are important, individual temperament remains the most critical factor in guide dog selection. Even within a breed known for its suitability as a guide dog, temperament can vary widely from dog to dog. Some dogs may have the right temperament for guide work, while others may not be suited for the challenges of the job.

Temperament assessments are a key part of the selection process. Dogs that display signs of fearfulness, anxiety, or aggression may not make good guide dogs, even if they come from a well-suited breed. The temperament evaluation ensures that only the most stable and reliable dogs are selected.

10. Future Trends in Breed Selection

As guide dog programs continue to evolve, there is growing interest in diversifying the gene pool to meet a wider range of client needs. Research into genetic testing, behavioral genetics, and emerging health data will continue to inform breeding practices. Advances in these fields may lead to new insights into which breeds and individual dogs are best suited for guide dog work.

Programs are also exploring the use of alternative breeds, such as smaller dogs for individuals who may not be able to handle larger dogs. The future of guide dog breeding looks promising, with new technologies and research helping to refine the selection process.

Conclusion

Selecting the right breed is crucial in guide dog training. The best guide dog breeds are those that possess intelligence, trainability, and an adaptable temperament. Labrador Retrievers, Golden Retrievers, and their crosses dominate the field due to their consistent success, but other breeds such as German Shepherds, Poodles, and Boxers have shown that diverse options can also be highly effective. Ultimately, while breed traits offer guidelines, individual temperament is the most important consideration. As guide dog programs continue to advance, the future will see even more refined breed selection processes, ensuring that the right dog is matched with the right client.

CHAPTER FOUR

The Science of Breeding and

Genetics in Guide Dogs

Introduction

The process of breeding guide dogs is both an art and a science. It requires a deep understanding of genetics, temperament, and health traits to ensure that the offspring will be suited for the demanding role of assisting people with visual impairments. In the past, guide dog programs relied largely on experience and intuition when selecting breeding pairs. However, advances in genetic research, as well as a greater understanding of dog behavior and health, have allowed these programs to make more informed and precise decisions. This chapter explores the science behind breeding guide dogs, how genetics plays a key role in their suitability for guide work, and how modern breeding techniques are evolving to ensure the best possible outcomes for both the dogs and the individuals they serve.

Understanding the genetic basis of guide dog suitability involves exploring traits such as intelligence, temperament, physical health, and even disease resistance. Additionally, the selection of breeding pairs based on genetic compatibility can help reduce hereditary health problems and increase the longevity and effectiveness of guide dogs. We will examine the key factors that guide dog breeding programs consider when selecting dogs for breeding and the role genetics plays in producing the ideal guide dog.

1. Genetic Traits that Impact Guide Dog Suitability

Genetics plays a pivotal role in determining a dog's suitability for guide dog work. Several traits are essential in selecting dogs that will thrive in the demanding role of guiding people with visual impairments. These traits are both inherited and influenced by the environment, but understanding their genetic underpinnings is key to successful breeding practices.

Key Traits:

- **Intelligence:** A guide dog must be able to quickly learn and adapt to new commands and tasks. This requires a high degree of intelligence. Dogs with a high capacity for problem-solving and reasoning are more likely to excel in guide dog training. Genetic factors influence cognitive abilities, so selecting dogs with a history of intelligence in their lineage is critical.

- **Temperament:** A calm and steady temperament is essential for guide dogs. Dogs that are easily startled, overly energetic, or aggressive may not be suited for guide dog work. Genetics play a major role in temperament, with certain lines of dogs being known for their calm and patient nature. By selecting dogs with good temperaments, breeding programs can produce puppies that are more likely to succeed as guide dogs.

- **Trainability:** Dogs must be willing and eager to work. This requires a desire to please their handler and a strong work ethic, traits that can be influenced by genetics. A dog's ability to focus and stay on task in high-pressure environments is vital for guide dog work.

- **Health:** Physical health is essential for any working dog, and guide dogs are no exception. Genetic predispositions to conditions such as hip dysplasia, cataracts, and epilepsy can significantly impact a dog's suitability for work. Breeding programs carefully screen dogs for these conditions and aim to breed for health and longevity.

2. The Role of DNA Testing in Breeding Decisions

DNA testing has become a valuable tool for breeding guide dogs. By testing for specific genetic markers associated with diseases and traits, breeders can make more informed decisions about which dogs to pair.

This has led to more precise breeding strategies, reducing the likelihood of hereditary health issues and ensuring that puppies will have the qualities necessary to excel as guide dogs.

Applications of DNA Testing:

- **Health Screening:** DNA testing allows breeders to screen for genetic disorders that are common in certain breeds. For example, Labrador Retrievers are prone to hip dysplasia, while Golden Retrievers are at higher risk for certain types of cancer. By identifying these conditions early, breeders can avoid pairing dogs that carry genetic markers for these disorders.

- **Temperament Markers:** Some studies have suggested that certain genes may influence temperament traits, such as anxiety or aggressiveness. By selecting dogs with desirable genetic markers for temperament, breeders can increase the likelihood of producing guide dogs with calm and steady dispositions.

- **Trainability Genes:** While it's difficult to pinpoint specific genes that influence trainability, genetic studies have identified certain traits that contribute to a dog's ability to learn and follow commands. By selecting dogs with a high potential for trainability, breeders can increase the odds of producing successful guide dogs.

- **Genetic Diversity:** One of the main goals of DNA testing is to maintain genetic diversity in breeding programs. By avoiding inbreeding and selecting genetically diverse pairs, breeders can reduce the risk of genetic problems and improve the overall health and well-being of the dog population.

DNA testing is an invaluable tool that allows breeders to make data-driven decisions, which in turn improves the overall success rate of guide dog programs.

3. Inbreeding and Genetic Diversity

While breeding dogs with desirable traits is crucial, it's equally important to maintain genetic diversity within the population of guide dogs. Inbreeding, which occurs when closely related dogs are bred, can increase the risk of genetic disorders and health problems. It can also reduce the overall vigor of the breed, making the dogs more susceptible to diseases.

The Importance of Genetic Diversity:

- **Health and Longevity:** Maintaining a diverse gene pool helps to prevent the accumulation of harmful genetic mutations. Dogs that come from a genetically diverse lineage are less likely to inherit serious health conditions and are more likely to live longer, healthier lives.

- **Physical and Behavioral Traits:** A diverse gene pool can also lead to a broader range of desirable physical and behavioral traits. For example, dogs from diverse backgrounds may have a better combination of intelligence, trainability, and temperament, making them more adaptable to different environments and training programs.

Breeding programs that prioritize genetic diversity are better equipped to produce guide dogs that meet the various needs of individuals with visual impairments. By using genetic testing to carefully select breeding pairs, these programs can avoid the pitfalls of inbreeding and ensure that the dogs they produce are strong, healthy, and well-suited for the job.

4. The Role of Environmental Factors

While genetics play a significant role in a dog's development, environmental factors also have a major impact. From the time a puppy is born, it undergoes a series of developmental stages that are influenced by its environment. Early socialization, exposure to different stimuli, and training experiences all shape a dog's behavior and temperament.

Key Environmental Factors:

- **Early Socialization**: The first few weeks of a puppy's life are crucial for its development. Puppies that are exposed to various people, other dogs, and different environments during this period are more likely to grow up well-adjusted and confident. Guide dog programs invest heavily in early socialization to ensure that puppies are comfortable in different settings and with a variety of stimuli.

- **Training and Experience:** While some dogs have an innate ability to learn and follow commands, training is still essential for guide dog work. Puppies that are raised in environments that encourage learning and problem-solving are more likely to excel in guide dog training. Positive reinforcement and consistency are key to shaping a dog's behavior and ensuring it learns the necessary skills to assist its handler.

- **Handler Compatibility:** Some dogs may perform better with specific handlers, depending on the handler's personality, energy level, and needs. Matching dogs with handlers who complement their behavior and needs is a crucial aspect of guide dog training. Breeding programs often work with trainers to assess each dog's compatibility with different types of handlers.

While genetics are crucial, the environment in which a dog is raised and trained plays an equally important role in determining its success as a guide dog.

5. Breeding for Specific Roles

Not all guide dogs are suited for the same roles. Some individuals may require a guide dog with a higher level of energy and assertiveness, while others may need a dog that is more laid-back and calm. Breeding programs may select specific traits based on the roles the dog will play, ensuring that each guide dog is well-suited for its intended purpose.

Different Roles in Guide Dog Work:

- **Urban Guide Dogs:** These dogs are required to navigate busy city streets, including intersections, crowded sidewalks, and public transportation. Urban guide dogs must be highly focused, calm in the face of distractions, and able to handle unpredictable situations. Breeding programs may select dogs that show high levels of trainability and resilience to stress for this role.

- **Rural Guide Dogs:** In more rural environments, guide dogs may need to help their handlers navigate open spaces, uneven terrain, and less structured environments. These dogs may need to be more independent and resourceful, able to think critically in less predictable situations.

- **Specialized Roles:** Some guide dogs are trained for specific roles, such as assisting handlers in airports or working in environments with a high level of noise or sensory overload. Breeding programs may select dogs with specific traits, such as a higher tolerance for noise or a more focused nature, for these roles.

6. Ethical Considerations in Guide Dog Breeding

Ethical considerations are integral to the breeding process in guide dog programs. It is essential to prioritize the well-being of the dogs and ensure that they are bred for the purpose of serving individuals with visual impairments, rather than for commercial gain. Ethical breeding practices focus on producing healthy, well-adjusted dogs that are capable of performing their duties without compromising their health or quality of life.

Key Ethical Principles:

- **Humane Treatment:** Guide dog breeders must ensure that the dogs are treated humanely throughout their lives. This includes proper care during pregnancy, socialization, and training, as well as providing adequate medical care.

- **Long-Term Welfare:** Ethical breeders consider the long-term welfare of the dogs, including their emotional and physical needs. This includes ensuring that dogs are not overworked or exposed to unnecessary stress, and that they are given the opportunity to live happy, fulfilling lives once they retire from their guide dog roles.

- **Avoiding Exploitation:** Breeding programs must avoid exploiting dogs for financial gain or other unethical purposes. Dogs should only be bred when there is a genuine need for guide dogs, and their welfare should always come first.

7. Future Trends in Guide Dog Breeding

Advancements in genetic research and breeding practices are continually improving the selection of guide dogs. As our understanding of genetics and behavioral science improves, breeding programs are better able to identify desirable traits and reduce the risk of hereditary health issues. Furthermore, emerging technologies, such as genetic editing, may open new possibilities for improving the health and effectiveness of guide dogs in the future.

Key Future Trends:

- **Genetic Engineering:** As genetic technologies continue to advance, researchers may be able to use genetic engineering techniques to eliminate hereditary diseases from dog populations. This could lead to healthier, more durable guide dogs that require fewer medical interventions.

- **Behavioral Genetics**: Future breeding programs may increasingly focus on behavioral genetics, identifying specific genes associated with traits like anxiety, aggression, and adaptability. This could allow for the more precise selection of dogs suited for guide work.

- **Crossbreeding and Hybrid Vigor:** The use of crossbreeding to create dogs that combine the best traits of different breeds may continue to grow, especially as new breeds are introduced into guide dog programs. This could lead to healthier and more adaptable guide dogs with better overall health and longevity.

Conclusion

The science of breeding and genetics plays a crucial role in producing the best guide dogs for individuals with visual impairments. By understanding the genetic basis of important traits like intelligence, temperament, and health, guide dog programs can make more informed decisions about breeding pairs. Through DNA testing, careful selection, and the application of ethical principles, breeding programs are able to create dogs that are well-suited to guide work and can lead long, healthy lives. As research continues to advance, the future of guide dog breeding looks promising, with more efficient and precise methods ensuring the continued success of guide dogs worldwide.

CHAPTER FIVE

A History of Guide Dogs

Introduction

The history of guide dogs is a remarkable journey, one that spans centuries and reflects the evolving relationship between humans and animals. Guide dogs, also known as seeing-eye dogs, have become an indispensable tool for individuals with visual impairments, but their journey to becoming the trusted companions they are today is rooted in a complex mix of compassion, ingenuity, and a shared desire for independence. This chapter delves into the rich tapestry of guide dog history, tracing its origins from ancient civilizations through to the modern-day guide dog programs that assist people all over the world.

Drawing from reputable sources and best-selling literature, we will explore the early uses of dogs for assistance, the formation of guide dog training programs, and the significant milestones in the development of guide dogs. Along the way, we will highlight key figures, organizations, and events that have shaped the history of guide dogs, emphasizing their enduring legacy as symbols of partnership, loyalty, and independence for people with visual impairments.

1. Early Use of Dogs for Assistance

The relationship between humans and dogs has been one of mutual benefit for thousands of years. Early civilizations recognized the utility of dogs in various roles, including herding, guarding, and hunting. However, it was not until much later in history that dogs were specifically trained to assist people with visual impairments.

In ancient cultures, dogs were occasionally seen accompanying individuals with disabilities, though they were not formally trained for this purpose. Ancient Egyptian artwork, for instance, depicts individuals with vision impairments walking with dogs, but it is unclear whether these dogs were specifically trained for guiding or simply served as companions. Similarly, in ancient Greece and Rome, there are references to blind individuals being accompanied by dogs, though formal guide dog training was not yet a concept.

While the idea of using dogs to assist those with visual impairments was recognized in ancient times, it wasn't until the 18th and 19th centuries that efforts to formally train dogs for guide work began to take shape.

2. The Role of Guide Dogs in the Early 20th Century

The modern history of guide dogs begins in the early 20th century, a time when a growing awareness of the needs of individuals with visual impairments led to increased efforts to provide more independence and mobility. During this period, a few pioneering individuals and organizations began experimenting with training dogs to assist the blind, laying the groundwork for the formal guide dog programs that would emerge later.

In the 1910s, Dr. Gerhard Stalling, a German ophthalmologist, is credited with being one of the first to recognize the potential for dogs to assist the visually impaired. Dr. Stalling worked at the Royal Prussian Institute for the Blind, where he developed the idea of training dogs to guide blind individuals. In 1916, he began his experiments with guiding dogs, using German Shepherds to assist visually impaired patients in moving around. This was an early attempt to apply canine assistance in a structured way, though the concept was not widely known at the time.

However, it was in the aftermath of World War I that guide dogs truly gained recognition. The war led to a large number of soldiers returning home with vision impairments due to injuries sustained on the battlefield. As a result, the need for mobility assistance became more apparent than ever before, and guide dogs became seen as a potential solution.

In 1916, the first successful training program for guide dogs was established in Germany, with the formation of the first guide dog school, the German Guide Dog School for the Blind. This school, established by Dr. Gerhard Stalling, formally trained dogs to help blind individuals navigate their environment, marking a significant milestone in the history of guide dogs.

3. The First Guide Dog School in America

Although Germany was the birthplace of formal guide dog training, it didn't take long for the idea to spread to other parts of the world. In the United States, the concept of guide dogs was introduced in the early 1920s, where it gained quick popularity due to the needs of returning veterans from World War I. It was in 1929 that the Seeing Eye organization was founded in the U.S. by Dorothy Harrison Eustis, a philanthropist, and Morris Frank, a blind man.

Dorothy Harrison Eustis, an American philanthropist and dog trainer, had been working with dogs in Switzerland when she became acquainted with a German guide dog program. Inspired by the success of the German model, she returned to the U.S. and, in collaboration with Morris Frank, established the first guide dog school in the country, The Seeing Eye in Morristown, New Jersey. Morris Frank, who became the first person to be paired with a guide dog in America, was instrumental in the development of the program. His enthusiasm for the new service dog quickly garnered public attention, and the organization began training dogs for visually impaired individuals across the country.

Morris Frank's story is one of the most significant in the history of guide dogs. Frank, who had been blind since childhood, struggled with navigating the world until he was paired with his first guide dog, Buddy. The bond between Frank and Buddy was transformative, allowing him to navigate independently for the first time in his life. This partnership helped to spread awareness about guide dogs and served as a powerful advocate for the formal establishment of guide dog training programs in the U.S.

The success of The Seeing Eye school was pivotal in changing perceptions of blindness and independence, and it played a key role in popularizing the concept of guide dogs across America. It also marked the beginning of a global movement, as other countries began to adopt similar training programs for guide dogs.

4. The Growth of Guide Dog Programs Worldwide

Following the success of The Seeing Eye in the United States, guide dog programs began to spread across the world. In the years following World War I, countries like England, France, and Canada established their own guide dog schools, inspired by the success stories of blind veterans and their canine companions.

In 1934, the Guide Dogs for the Blind Association was founded in the United Kingdom by Dorothy Harrison Eustis, further cementing her legacy as a leader in the guide dog movement. This organization followed the principles laid out by The Seeing Eye and became one of the most well-known guide dog organizations in the world. The work done by the Guide Dogs for the Blind Association helped ensure that guide dogs became more widely available for individuals in the UK and beyond.

By the mid-20th century, the number of guide dog schools around the world had significantly increased. These schools developed different approaches to training, each with its own curriculum and philosophies, but all shared the same goal: to provide blind individuals with the means to navigate their world independently and confidently.

5. The Evolution of Guide Dog Training

Guide dog training has come a long way since the early days of the 20th century. As awareness of the needs of visually impaired individuals grew, so too did the sophistication of guide dog training methods. Early training focused primarily on teaching dogs basic commands, but over time, the process became much more refined.

Training today typically begins with selecting the right dog—usually a breed with specific traits such as intelligence, calmness, and physical stamina. Labrador Retrievers, Golden Retrievers, and German Shepherds are commonly chosen for their temperament and intelligence. Once a suitable dog is found, it undergoes an intensive training program that can last anywhere from 6 to 12 months.

The process involves teaching the dog to navigate urban and rural environments, avoid obstacles, and respond to the needs of its handler. During this time, the dog learns to follow cues such as "forward," "left," "right," "stop," and "harness," and is exposed to various situations to ensure that it can perform under a variety of conditions. Additionally, socialization is a key part of the training, as guide dogs need to remain calm and focused despite the distractions that might occur in busy environments.

Training is often a collaborative effort between the dog and its handler, with the dog and handler working together to build trust and understanding. This relationship is foundational to the success of the partnership, as the handler depends on the dog to guide them safely through the world.

6. Guide Dogs Today: Advancements and Challenges

Today, guide dogs continue to serve as vital tools for people with visual impairments, enabling them to navigate the world independently. There are now more than 70 guide dog schools around the world, and the number of guide dogs trained annually continues to rise. Advances in veterinary care, training techniques, and technology have all contributed to improving the success rate and quality of guide dog partnerships.

However, despite these advancements, there are still challenges to overcome. Demand for guide dogs often outpaces supply, leading to long waiting lists for individuals who need them. Additionally, guide dog organizations face funding and resource challenges as they continue to grow and expand. The rising cost of breeding, training, and caring for guide dogs also remains a concern for many organizations.

Moreover, guide dogs are not just working dogs—they are also companions. The bond between a guide dog and its handler is often described as life-changing, with many handlers referring to their dogs as family members. This emotional connection adds an important layer to the work guide dogs do, as they are not just navigating the world for their handlers but providing comfort, companionship, and support.

7. The Future of Guide Dogs

As guide dog programs continue to evolve, there are exciting prospects on the horizon. Emerging technologies such as GPS tracking, smart collars, and wearable devices are being integrated into guide dog programs to improve navigation and safety. These technologies can help enhance the relationship between guide dogs and their handlers, offering additional layers of support while maintaining the trust and partnership at the heart of the guide dog experience.

Genetic research is also likely to play an increasing role in the breeding and training of guide dogs, ensuring that dogs with the best traits are selected for the job. This will continue to improve the efficiency and health of guide dogs, further solidifying their place as vital tools for independence.

Conclusion

The history of guide dogs is a testament to the power of innovation, compassion, and dedication. From ancient civilizations to the modern-day organizations that train them, guide dogs have played a crucial role in the lives of people with visual impairments. Through their training, commitment, and companionship, guide dogs continue to help individuals achieve a sense of independence and freedom that was once thought impossible. The journey of guide dogs is far from over, and as technology and training methods evolve, their legacy will continue to grow, providing hope and assistance to countless individuals worldwide.

CHAPTER SIX

The Process of Training Guide Dogs

Introduction

The training of guide dogs is a rigorous and complex process, one that demands patience, skill, and understanding of both the dog's and the handler's needs. The training is not simply about teaching a dog to follow commands; it's about creating a partnership based on mutual trust, clear communication, and the development of skills that enable a person with a visual impairment to navigate the world with confidence and independence. This chapter will explore the detailed steps involved in training guide dogs, from selecting the right dog to the eventual pairing with a visually impaired individual. We will also examine the challenges and breakthroughs that have shaped guide dog training techniques over the years.

Drawing on best-selling literature and reputable sources, this chapter will provide a thorough overview of the training process, showcasing the critical phases of training, the role of trainers, and the relationship between guide dogs and their handlers.

1. Selecting the Right Dog

The first step in training a guide dog is selecting a suitable dog. Not every dog is suited for guide dog work, and careful consideration must be given to various factors such as temperament, health, and physical traits. The ideal guide dog needs to have a calm temperament, high intelligence, excellent socialization skills, and the ability to concentrate in busy environments.

1.1. Ideal Breeds for Guide Dogs

While many breeds can potentially be trained as guide dogs, some are better suited to the task than others. The most common breeds used for guide dogs are Labrador Retrievers, Golden Retrievers, and German

Shepherds. These breeds are chosen for their gentle temperament, strong work ethic, intelligence, and physical capabilities.

Labrador Retrievers are often considered the gold standard for guide dogs due to their friendly nature, eagerness to please, and ease of training.

Golden Retrievers share similar traits to Labrador Retrievers, including their gentle nature and willingness to work alongside their handlers.

German Shepherds are known for their intelligence, alertness, and ability to handle more complex tasks. They are often used for guide dog work in more demanding environments, where a higher level of focus and endurance is required.

Less commonly, breeds such as Standard Poodles, Belgian Malinois, and Flat-Coated Retrievers have also been trained as guide dogs, though these are less prevalent due to breed-specific challenges.

1.2. Health and Temperament Considerations

Health and temperament are critical factors when selecting a guide dog. Dogs chosen for guide dog training must be in excellent health, free from genetic conditions or diseases that could impair their performance. Most guide dog organizations conduct thorough health screenings to ensure that dogs are physically capable of enduring the training process.

Temperament is perhaps the most important consideration. Guide dogs must be calm, steady, and confident, even in crowded or noisy environments. They should not be easily distracted, frightened, or overly excitable, as these traits can hinder their ability to perform their duties effectively. Additionally, guide dogs should be highly social and comfortable interacting with people and other dogs.

2. Puppy Development and Early Training

Once a dog has been selected for guide dog training, it begins a developmental process that lasts for several months, typically starting when the dog is around 8 weeks old. The early stages of training focus on socialization, basic obedience, and introducing the dog to various environments to help them build confidence.

2.1. Socialization

Socialization is one of the most important aspects of early training. During this stage, the puppy is exposed to a wide range of environments, sounds, smells, and people. The goal is to ensure that the puppy grows up to be confident, well-adjusted, and able to handle a variety of distractions without becoming stressed or anxious.

Puppies are also introduced to different objects and surfaces, such as traffic noises, busy streets, escalators, and public transportation. Exposure to such environments helps prepare the dog for the complexities of guiding its handler in real-world situations.

2.2. Basic Obedience Training

Basic obedience is the foundation of guide dog training. Puppies learn essential commands such as "sit," "stay," "down," and "come." These commands are critical for establishing communication between the dog and its future handler, as they will be used throughout the training process and in everyday situations.

Additionally, puppies begin to learn more complex behaviors, such as walking on a loose leash, not pulling on the lead, and walking calmly next to a person. They are also trained to become accustomed to wearing a harness, which will be used during the guide dog training stages to direct them when guiding their handler.

3. Formal Guide Dog Training

The formal guide dog training program typically begins when the dog is between 12 and 18 months old. By this point, the dog has completed its early socialization and basic obedience training. The goal of formal training is to teach the dog the specific skills needed to guide a visually impaired person safely and effectively.

3.1. Orientation and Mobility Training

The foundation of guide dog training is orientation and mobility (O&M). O&M training focuses on teaching the dog to guide its handler in various environments, navigate obstacles, and avoid hazards. The dog is trained to follow specific commands from the trainer, such as "left," "right," "forward," and "stop."

During this phase, the guide dog learns to respond to environmental cues and to guide its handler around obstacles such as curbs, traffic, and people. The dog is taught to recognize different types of terrain and respond accordingly, whether it's a narrow sidewalk, a busy street, or an open space.

The dog must also learn to stop at intersections, find doors, and even help its handler avoid obstacles such as street furniture or uneven pavement. Throughout this phase, trainers use positive reinforcement techniques, rewarding the dog for correct behavior with treats and praise.

3.2. Environmental Distractions

Training in real-world environments is crucial to guide dog success. The dog must be able to guide its handler in a variety of challenging settings, such as busy city streets, shopping malls, public transportation, and airports. Training is conducted in a variety of environments to expose the dog to different distractions, such as other people, vehicles, loud noises, and unfamiliar smells.

Guide dog trainers also simulate potentially hazardous situations, such as sudden changes in traffic patterns, moving crowds, and weather conditions. By training in these environments, the dog learns to stay focused on its task and ignore distractions, which is vital for guiding its handler safely and confidently.

3.3. Command Refinement and Responsiveness

As the dog progresses through its training, trainers focus on refining the dog's responsiveness to commands. The dog must become adept at recognizing and responding to subtle cues, such as slight tugs on the harness or a change in the handler's posture. These cues help the dog interpret the handler's needs and anticipate their next move.

Additionally, the dog must learn to adapt to its handler's individual walking style and pace. Some handlers may walk more quickly, while others may move more slowly, so the dog must be flexible in its approach to guiding. This phase of training emphasizes precision, ensuring that the dog is capable of guiding its handler safely and efficiently in any situation.

4. Pairing the Dog with Its Handler

Once the dog has completed its formal training, it is time to pair the dog with a visually impaired person. This is a critical phase of the process, as the dog must form a strong bond with its handler and learn how to work as a team. The pairing process can take several weeks and involves intensive training with the handler to establish trust and communication.

4.1. Introduction to the Handler

The introduction to the handler begins with familiarization. The handler gets to know the dog in a controlled environment, where both can build rapport and establish a comfortable relationship. During this time, the handler works with the dog to practice basic commands and learn how to communicate effectively.

The pairing process also involves training the handler to use the dog's harness and work with the dog in different environments. The handler is taught how to give appropriate commands, how to respond to the dog's cues, and how to maintain control during walks. This phase is also a time for the handler to build confidence in their ability to work with the dog, as the dog learns to understand and respond to the handler's needs.

4.2. Teamwork and Confidence Building

The final step of pairing involves building teamwork and confidence. The handler and dog work together in real-world scenarios, navigating streets, crossing intersections, and avoiding obstacles. Over time, the bond between the handler and the dog deepens, and both learn to rely on each other for safety and direction.

Throughout this phase, the trainer provides support, helping the handler and dog refine their teamwork. The trainer also monitors the dog's behavior to ensure that it continues to perform at a high level. This period often marks the transition from formal training to independent work, as the handler and dog begin to work together seamlessly.

5. Ongoing Training and Support

Even after the dog is paired with its handler, the training process does not end. Guide dogs require ongoing training and maintenance to ensure that they continue to meet the needs of their handlers and to keep their skills sharp. This often involves periodic check-ins with the training organization, where the dog's performance is assessed and any necessary adjustments are made.

Additionally, many organizations provide ongoing support for handlers, offering assistance with dog care, maintenance, and troubleshooting any issues that may arise. Guide dog teams are encouraged to attend refresher courses and engage in continued learning to maintain the bond and effectiveness of their partnership.

Conclusion

The training of guide dogs is a dynamic, complex, and rewarding process that involves careful selection, early socialization, rigorous formal training, and a strong partnership between the dog and its handler. This process requires a team effort from breeders, trainers, and handlers to ensure that guide dogs are fully equipped to assist individuals with visual impairments in navigating the world safely and confidently. As technology, training methods, and research continue to evolve, so too will the training process, ensuring that future guide dog teams are better equipped to handle the challenges of tomorrow.

CHAPTER SEVEN

Guide Dogs in Action: Real-Life Stories of Empowerment and Independence

Introduction

The true power of guide dogs lies in the profound impact they have on the lives of individuals with visual impairments. While the training and techniques involved in preparing guide dogs are critical, the real magic happens when these dogs are paired with their handlers, providing them with the confidence, safety, and independence they need to navigate the world. This chapter will explore real-life stories of individuals who have been empowered by their guide dogs, highlighting the importance of this partnership in transforming lives. By examining the experiences of guide dog users, we will understand the true role of guide dogs as not just service animals, but as companions, protectors, and life-changing assets.

Drawing from reputable sources and best-selling literature, we will delve into inspiring stories, illustrating how guide dogs have helped individuals overcome daily challenges, develop a sense of autonomy, and, ultimately, thrive in a world that often feels inaccessible without the support of a guide dog.

1. The Journey of Empowerment

1.1. Overcoming the Obstacles of Vision Loss

For many individuals with visual impairments, the path to independence is fraught with obstacles, both physical and emotional. Vision loss can be an isolating experience, and the inability to navigate public spaces independently often leaves people feeling vulnerable and confined to the safety of their homes. However, the introduction of a guide dog can dramatically alter this reality. By providing not only the physical support necessary to navigate the world but also a deep emotional connection, guide dogs empower their handlers to regain control of their lives.

Take the story of Maria, a woman in her 30s who lost her vision due to a degenerative condition. Prior to receiving her guide dog, Maria found herself relying on family members and public transportation, both of which made her feel dependent and frustrated. The loss of her independence was difficult, but when she was paired with a Labrador Retriever named Buddy, everything changed.

Buddy was not only able to help Maria navigate busy streets but also boosted her confidence in unfamiliar environments. With Buddy by her side, Maria was able to regain a sense of normalcy. She no longer needed to depend on others for daily tasks like grocery shopping or commuting to work. Through her relationship with Buddy, Maria found new strength, enabling her to embrace her independence and lead a fulfilling life.

1.2. The Lifelong Bond

The relationship between a guide dog and its handler goes beyond the practicalities of guiding; it is a lifelong bond built on trust, communication, and affection. Guide dogs are not simply trained to assist with mobility— they are also trained to be emotionally attuned to their handler's needs. The presence of a guide dog provides its handler with emotional stability, companionship, and a sense of security that cannot be underestimated.

James, a man who has been visually impaired since birth, shared how his guide dog, Echo, gave him the emotional support that he had never fully realized he needed. Prior to receiving Echo, James often felt isolated, as he was hesitant to interact with people in public due to the fear of not being able to navigate unfamiliar places. Echo's gentle and intuitive nature helped James feel less anxious and more comfortable in social settings.

James's experience illustrates how guide dogs not only assist with physical mobility but also foster emotional well-being. The dog's presence reassures its handler that they are never truly alone, enabling them to pursue life with a renewed sense of optimism and freedom.

2. Overcoming Public Perception and Misunderstandings

2.1. Breaking Down Barriers in Society

Despite the transformative impact of guide dogs, many individuals with visual impairments still face significant barriers when it comes to public perception and societal acceptance. Misunderstandings about the role of guide dogs often result in challenges in public spaces, whether it's people who try to distract the dog or businesses that are not aware of their legal responsibilities regarding service animals.

One inspiring story is that of Samantha, a young professional who was paired with a Golden Retriever named Daisy. After experiencing her first few weeks with Daisy, Samantha found herself facing the challenge of public misunderstanding. On several occasions, people attempted to pet Daisy or engage her in conversation, unaware that Daisy was working. While the intentions were often kind, these interruptions could distract Daisy from her task and compromise Samantha's safety.

Through education and advocacy, Samantha became a passionate voice for guide dog awareness. She began educating those around her about the importance of not distracting guide dogs and the rights that people with visual impairments have when it comes to access to public spaces. Samantha's story is a powerful reminder that while guide dogs can make a world of difference, there is still work to be done in educating the public and removing barriers for individuals with disabilities.

2.2. Legal Protections and Rights

In many countries, guide dogs are protected under laws that grant people with visual impairments the right to bring their guide dogs into public spaces, including restaurants, hotels, and public transportation. These laws are designed to ensure that individuals with visual impairments can live independently without encountering unnecessary discrimination.

In the United States, the Americans with Disabilities Act (ADA) provides strong legal protections for individuals who rely on service animals, including guide dogs. Despite these protections, individuals like Carlos, a blind man living in a busy city, continue to face challenges. On one occasion, Carlos was asked to leave a coffee shop because the manager mistakenly believed that only "trained service animals" were allowed. However, Carlos was able to assert his legal rights and educate the manager, ultimately resolving the situation. Carlos's story highlights the importance of knowing one's rights and advocating for the inclusion of guide dogs in all public spaces.

3. Guide Dogs in Specific Environments

3.1. Navigating Urban Landscapes

Cities can present a daunting environment for someone with a visual impairment. From busy streets filled with traffic to crowded public transportation systems, navigating the urban landscape requires careful planning and preparation. Guide dogs are instrumental in helping individuals confidently move through these environments, overcoming challenges such as uneven sidewalks, street crossings, and navigating through busy crowds.

Rachel, a city dweller, shares her experience of moving to a bustling metropolis after receiving her guide dog, Baxter. Having lived in a rural area prior to her move, Rachel was apprehensive about navigating a large city on her own. However, Baxter proved to be more than capable of handling the challenges of urban life. From guiding her safely through subway stations to helping her find the entrance to her favorite café, Baxter became her trusted guide in an environment that once seemed overwhelming.

Guide dogs like Baxter are specifically trained to handle complex urban environments, providing their handlers with the security they need to live, work, and play in cities across the globe.

3.2. Navigating Rural and Outdoor Environments

While cities are often associated with challenges for guide dogs, rural areas and outdoor environments also require specific skills. Guide dogs need to be able to navigate uneven terrain, rural streets, and even outdoor trails. For individuals who enjoy hiking, running, or spending time outdoors, having a guide dog trained to handle such environments is a game-changer.

Take the story of David, an avid outdoorsman who, after losing his vision, thought his love for nature would be permanently curtailed. However, after being paired with Juno, a highly trained guide dog, David was able to return to the hiking trails he once loved. Juno not only guided him through forests and parks but also helped David find his way on nature trails that were sometimes uneven and challenging. This story highlights the versatility of guide dogs and their ability to adapt to both urban and natural environments, offering their handlers the freedom to enjoy a wide range of experiences.

4. The Importance of Continued Support

4.1. Lifelong Training and Adaptation

Guide dog teams do not stop working once the initial training is complete. As their handlers' needs change over time, continued support and training are crucial to ensuring the ongoing success of the partnership. Guide dog organizations often offer lifelong support, including periodic check-ins, refresher courses, and the ability to request assistance if the team encounters any challenges.

Clara, a guide dog handler for over a decade, shared her experience of transitioning into a new phase of life when her mobility needs changed. With the support of her guide dog's training organization, Clara was able to receive additional training, adapting her routine and ensuring that she and her dog, Milo, could continue to work effectively together. This story demonstrates the importance of ongoing support, ensuring that guide dog teams can continue to thrive even as their needs evolve.

Conclusion

The real-life stories of guide dog users showcase the incredible potential of these animals to transform lives. Whether navigating crowded city streets, reclaiming lost independence, or providing emotional support, guide dogs play an indispensable role in the lives of those who rely on them. The empowerment that guide dogs provide is not just physical but emotional and psychological as well. As these stories demonstrate, the bond between a guide dog and its handler is built on trust, teamwork, and mutual respect, ultimately enabling people to live fuller, more independent lives.

CHAPTER EIGHT

The Training Process: From Puppy to Guide Dog

Introduction

The journey from a puppy to a fully trained guide dog is both rigorous and rewarding. Guide dog training is a carefully structured process that requires patience, skill, and consistency. The training not only ensures that the dog has the physical ability to assist its handler in navigating the world but also fosters a deep bond between the dog and its human partner. In this chapter, we will explore the detailed training process that guide dogs undergo, starting from their early days as puppies, all the way through to their specialized training and final partnership with a handler.

Drawing on expert knowledge, reputable sources, and best-selling literature, this chapter delves into each stage of the training process, discussing the key elements that contribute to a guide dog's success. The training process is as much about forming a relationship of trust between the dog and its future handler as it is about developing the skills necessary to perform vital tasks. Through this detailed examination, we will gain a greater appreciation for the immense work involved in producing a service dog that changes lives.

1. Early Development: The First Weeks of Life

1.1. The Role of Breeding in Early Development

The first stage of guide dog training begins long before the dog even meets its future handler. The initial months of a guide dog's life are crucial for shaping its temperament and character. The breeding process for guide dogs involves selecting dogs with certain desirable traits, such as intelligence, temperament, and physical health. The aim is to ensure that the puppy will grow into a dog capable of performing the demanding tasks required of a guide dog.

Dogs selected for guide dog training often come from a specific set of breeds that are known for their trainability and suitability for service work. Breeds such as Labrador Retrievers, Golden Retrievers, and German Shepherds are commonly chosen for guide dog training due to their intelligence, patience, and temperament. These breeds are also physically strong, which is essential for the work they will eventually do.

In the early weeks of life, puppies are cared for in a nurturing environment that fosters their physical and emotional development. While they are still with their mothers, they are exposed to a variety of stimuli, including socialization with other puppies, sounds, and textures. Early socialization is crucial for ensuring that the dog will be comfortable in a variety of environments once it begins its formal training.

1.2. Puppy Raisers: The First Step in Training

After the first few weeks of life, puppies are typically placed with puppy raisers, who are volunteers trained to care for and raise the puppies until they are ready for formal training. These raisers play an essential role in the early development of the puppies, teaching them basic obedience commands, house training, and introducing them to a variety of situations that will help them adapt to the diverse environments they will encounter as guide dogs.

Puppy raisers expose their foster dogs to different types of people, animals, and environments to help the puppies develop the confidence and social skills they will need to work with a visually impaired person. They also begin teaching the dogs basic commands such as "sit," "stay," and "come," which will form the foundation for more advanced training later on.

The role of a puppy raiser is demanding yet rewarding. These individuals help shape the future of a guide dog by instilling the values of obedience, patience, and socialization in the dogs, giving them the best chance at becoming successful working animals.

2. Formal Training: From Obedience to Specialization

2.1. Advanced Obedience Training

Once a guide dog reaches an appropriate age—usually around 12 to 18 months—it begins its formal training. This phase is typically conducted by professional trainers at a guide dog school or training facility. The goal of this stage is to reinforce the obedience commands that the dog has already learned and to teach the dog more advanced skills that will help it assist a person with visual impairments.

The training process begins with building on the basic obedience skills the dog has already mastered. The dog learns to respond consistently to commands such as "sit," "stay," "heel," and "come." These commands form the foundation of the dog's behavior, ensuring that it can follow directions with precision when working with its handler.

One key aspect of advanced obedience training is teaching the dog to focus on its handler at all times. A guide dog must be attuned to its handler's needs and be able to make quick decisions in dynamic environments. During this phase of training, the dog learns to ignore distractions such as other people, other animals, or noises that might occur in its surroundings. This skill is essential, as guide dogs must be able to maintain focus on their handler's movements and commands, ensuring the safety and efficiency of their work.

2.2. Learning to Guide: The Critical Mobility Skills

The most important part of a guide dog's training is learning how to guide its handler safely through various environments. This phase of training involves teaching the dog to navigate obstacles, find curbs and street crossings, and safely guide its handler through busy or complex areas such as shopping malls, public transportation stations, or city streets.

Guide dogs are trained to stop at curbs, lead their handlers safely around obstacles, and make decisions based on the handler's movements. For example, if a guide dog encounters an obstacle such as a parked car, it is trained to lead the handler around the obstacle to the safest path. The dog is also trained to avoid dangerous situations, such as stopping at a crosswalk and waiting for the signal to change before guiding the handler across the street.

The training process emphasizes the importance of ensuring the handler's safety at all times. Guide dogs learn to make split-second decisions to ensure that their handler's path is clear and that they avoid potential hazards, such as cars, uneven surfaces, or crowds of people.

2.3. Specialized Training for Complex Tasks

In addition to basic guiding skills, guide dogs are trained to perform more complex tasks. These may include guiding their handler to specific locations, opening doors, picking up dropped items, or even assisting with finding public facilities like restrooms. As part of their training, dogs are also taught to work in specific environments, such as airports, restaurants, or hospitals, where the nature of their work may require more specialized skills.

Some dogs may also receive additional training to help them navigate specific environments or perform specialized tasks. For instance, some guide dogs are trained to work in rural environments, where the terrain may be uneven or challenging. Others may be trained to work with handlers who have additional disabilities, such as hearing loss, requiring the dog to be attuned to different signals or needs.

The complexity and depth of the specialized training ensure that each guide dog is capable of handling the unique challenges it will face in real-world scenarios, adapting to its handler's needs and environment with precision and care.

3. Pairing with a Handler: The Final Stage of Training

3.1. The Matching Process

Once a guide dog has completed its training, the final stage of the process is the pairing with a handler. This is one of the most crucial steps in the guide dog training journey, as the success of the partnership depends on how well the dog and handler work together.

The matching process involves carefully assessing the needs of the individual handler, including their mobility level, lifestyle, and preferences. Trainers consider factors such as the handler's walking speed, whether they require additional assistance with tasks beyond mobility, and the environment in which they live. Based on these factors, the trainers select a dog that will complement the handler's needs and personality.

The pairing process also involves an initial training session in which the handler learns how to work with their new guide dog. This training often takes place at the guide dog school, where the handler is introduced to their dog and learns how to give commands, work with the dog, and build the necessary trust and communication. During this phase, both the dog and the handler undergo a period of adjustment as they learn to trust one another and work as a team.

3.2. The First Few Weeks with a New Guide Dog

The first few weeks with a new guide dog can be both exciting and challenging for the handler. It is a period of learning, communication, and trust-building. Handlers must learn to read their dog's cues, while the dog adjusts to its new handler's pace and movements.

During this period, the guide dog trainer will continue to monitor the progress of the team, providing support and guidance as needed. With time, the dog and handler become more attuned to one another, developing a deep and rewarding partnership that lasts for years.

4. Lifelong Learning and Support

4.1. Ongoing Support for the Guide Dog Team

The training process doesn't end once the dog is paired with its handler. Guide dog teams continue to receive support throughout their working life. Guide dog organizations offer ongoing training sessions, check-ins, and refresher courses to ensure that the team remains in sync and that the dog continues to work effectively.

In addition to formal training, guide dogs often receive medical care and regular assessments to ensure their health and well-being. Handlers can also contact the guide dog organization for support if they encounter challenges or require assistance with their dog's behavior or training.

4.2. Retirement and Transition

As guide dogs age, they may eventually retire from active service. This transition is carefully managed, with the handler often being involved in the decision-making process. Retired guide dogs are typically placed in loving homes, where they can enjoy a well-earned rest after years of dedicated service. Some handlers may choose to adopt their retired guide dog, maintaining the strong bond they developed during their working years.

Conclusion

The process of training a guide dog is a remarkable journey that involves time, patience, and dedication. From the early development stages to the pairing process, every step is designed to ensure that the dog can provide the highest level of assistance to its handler. Guide dogs not only provide physical support and mobility assistance but also offer emotional stability, companionship, and independence. Through this rigorous training process, guide dogs become invaluable partners in the lives of those they serve, empowering individuals with visual impairments to lead full and independent lives.

CHAPTER NINE

The Role of Guide Dogs in Improving

the Quality of Life

Introduction

Guide dogs play a vital role in enhancing the quality of life for people with visual impairments. Beyond the physical assistance they provide in navigating the world, guide dogs offer emotional, psychological, and social benefits that transform their handlers' daily experiences. The relationship between a guide dog and its handler is one of mutual trust, communication, and support. This chapter explores how guide dogs go beyond their practical functions to become integral partners in the lives of those they assist.

Drawing from reputable sources and expert insights, we will examine the various dimensions of how guide dogs improve the quality of life for individuals with visual impairments. From enhancing mobility to fostering independence and social integration, guide dogs make profound impacts on their handlers, improving not only their daily activities but also their overall well-being. We will also look at the broader societal impact of guide dogs, including how they help challenge perceptions about disability and contribute to a more inclusive world.

1. Enhancing Mobility and Independence

1.1. Navigating the World with Confidence

One of the primary functions of a guide dog is to assist its handler in navigating their environment safely and efficiently. For individuals who are blind or visually impaired, mobility can be a significant challenge. Guide dogs are trained to guide their handlers around obstacles, find curbs, and safely cross streets. However, their role goes beyond simply providing physical assistance; guide dogs enable their handlers to feel confident and independent as they navigate through the world.

For individuals without visual impairments, moving around the world is often a task taken for granted. For someone with a visual impairment, everyday activities like going to work, visiting a friend, or running errands can become overwhelming. Guide dogs reduce these challenges by offering safe, reliable navigation through potentially hazardous environments. By following cues from the dog, handlers can trust that they are being guided along the safest route, allowing them to move with confidence and independence.

This sense of mobility freedom is life-changing. Many individuals with visual impairments report a sense of empowerment and increased self-esteem after receiving a guide dog. With the dog as a constant companion, the feeling of being "trapped" or isolated due to vision loss diminishes. Guide dogs enable their handlers to engage in society with more confidence, increasing their ability to participate in daily life activities.

1.2. Removing Physical Barriers

Guide dogs also help remove physical barriers that can be especially challenging for individuals with visual impairments. In unfamiliar environments, such as a busy city street or a crowded public space, navigating can become dangerous and exhausting. Guide dogs are trained to stop at curbs, identify obstacles in the path, and guide the handler around them, allowing them to avoid potential accidents such as tripping, falling, or getting hit by vehicles.

Beyond the navigation of physical obstacles, guide dogs also assist in more nuanced tasks, such as identifying doorways or stairs, opening doors, and even locating public facilities like restrooms. These everyday tasks, which may seem small but are crucial for maintaining independence, become manageable with a guide dog by the handler's side.

The relationship between the handler and the guide dog extends beyond a functional partnership; it becomes a dependable support system. When working together, the bond between the dog and its handler becomes critical in providing both physical and emotional security, especially in unfamiliar or challenging situations.

2. Psychological and Emotional Benefits

2.1. Enhancing Mental Health

The psychological and emotional benefits of having a guide dog cannot be overstated. For individuals with visual impairments, the experience of blindness or low vision can sometimes lead to feelings of isolation, depression, and anxiety. The presence of a guide dog helps to alleviate many of these emotional challenges by providing a consistent source of companionship and support.

Guide dogs offer their handlers not only physical assistance but also emotional comfort. The companionship of a guide dog fosters a sense of connectedness and reduces feelings of loneliness. In many ways, the dog becomes a best friend, confidante, and emotional anchor for the individual. This relationship can lead to increased emotional stability, as the handler can rely on their guide dog to provide support during difficult moments or in emotionally stressful situations.

Studies have shown that pet ownership, in general, has a positive impact on mental health, reducing symptoms of anxiety and depression. For individuals with visual impairments, this effect is amplified, as the bond with a guide dog helps to restore a sense of independence, dignity, and emotional well-being. The dog's unwavering support can help the handler regain confidence in themselves and their abilities, which, in turn, has a positive effect on their mental health.

2.2. Promoting Social Interaction

Guide dogs also play a critical role in fostering social interactions. People with visual impairments may feel socially isolated due to the challenges of mobility and the stigma that often accompanies disability. A guide dog serves as a social bridge, helping the handler engage with others and feel more included in social settings.

The presence of a guide dog often attracts positive attention from others, sparking conversations and interactions that might not otherwise take place. People are generally more inclined to approach and interact with a person accompanied by a guide dog, creating opportunities for social connections and support networks. These interactions can be particularly important for people who may otherwise find it difficult to navigate social spaces or meet new people.

Moreover, the presence of a guide dog can help reduce the social stigma attached to visual impairments. By fostering positive social interactions, guide dogs help normalize disability and promote inclusivity. Their presence in public spaces allows individuals with visual impairments to feel more confident in social situations, thereby enhancing their sense of belonging and self-worth.

2.3. Restoring Dignity and Autonomy

Guide dogs play an essential role in restoring a sense of dignity and autonomy to individuals with visual impairments. In many ways, a guide dog is more than just a tool for mobility; it is a symbol of self-sufficiency and independence. For someone who may have struggled with the feeling of dependence due to their vision loss, a guide dog provides a tangible way to regain control over their daily life.

This restored independence is particularly important in a world that often views disability through a lens of limitation. A guide dog enables its handler to make independent decisions, such as choosing the best route to take or deciding when to cross the street. The handler no longer has to rely on others for assistance in everyday tasks but can instead rely on their guide dog to navigate the world with them.

The dignity that comes from having a guide dog is profound. It allows individuals with visual impairments to participate more fully in society, take on challenges, and perform tasks that they might have otherwise avoided. The guide dog serves as a constant reminder that independence and dignity are achievable, even in the face of disability.

3. Broader Societal Impact

3.1. Challenging Perceptions of Disability

Guide dogs play a significant role in challenging societal perceptions of disability. In many cultures, there is still a tendency to view people with disabilities as limited or dependent. However, the partnership between a guide dog and its handler showcases the immense capabilities of individuals with visual impairments.

The presence of guide dogs in public spaces helps to change attitudes towards disability by demonstrating that people with visual impairments can lead independent, active lives. Guide dogs empower their handlers to become contributing members of society, pursuing careers, education, and hobbies just like anyone else. This visibility and representation challenge the traditional narrative of disability and promote a more inclusive society.

By fostering independence and mobility, guide dogs show the world that disability does not equate to incapacity. They serve as a powerful reminder that with the right tools, support, and determination, people with disabilities can achieve their full potential.

3.2. Promoting Inclusion and Accessibility

Guide dogs also contribute to promoting inclusion and accessibility in society. As more individuals with visual impairments gain access to guide dogs, the need for accessible infrastructure and services becomes increasingly evident. Guide dogs are often at the forefront of advocating for accessible public spaces, including transportation, buildings, and outdoor areas.

Their presence highlights the importance of creating environments that are both physically and socially accessible to everyone, regardless of their abilities. As guide dogs lead their handlers through urban landscapes, they help to identify gaps in accessibility that need to be addressed. These gaps might include lack of tactile paving, poor lighting, or insufficient public transportation options.

In this way, guide dogs play a role in pushing for societal change. They contribute to a broader movement toward making the world more inclusive, ensuring that individuals with visual impairments can access and engage in all aspects of society without barriers.

4. The Lasting Bond: A Lifetime of Service

4.1. Building a Relationship of Trust

The bond between a guide dog and its handler is built on mutual trust, respect, and understanding. From the moment the dog is paired with its handler, the relationship begins to grow. This bond is crucial for ensuring the success of the partnership, as both the dog and the handler must rely on one another for support, guidance, and safety.

The bond between the dog and handler is not one-sided. While the guide

dog provides physical assistance, the handler offers love, care, and attention, ensuring that the dog remains healthy and happy. The mutual respect and trust that develop between the two create a strong foundation for the lifetime partnership that will unfold.

4.2. Retirement and Legacy

As guide dogs age, they eventually retire from active service. This transition is carefully managed to ensure that both the dog and the handler can adjust to this change. Retired guide dogs often continue to live with their handlers, maintaining the deep bond that they have formed over the years.

The legacy of a guide dog's service extends far beyond its active years. The memories, experiences, and shared moments between the dog and handler continue to shape their lives long after retirement. Many handlers choose to adopt their retired guide dogs, ensuring that the bond remains strong and that the dog can continue to live a fulfilling life in its later years.

Conclusion

Guide dogs have a profound and life-changing impact on the lives of individuals with visual impairments. Through their assistance, companionship, and support, guide dogs enhance their handlers' mobility, independence, emotional well-being, and social interactions. Their presence challenges societal perceptions of disability and promotes greater inclusivity and accessibility. The bond between a guide dog and its handler is one of deep trust and mutual respect, creating a partnership that lasts for a lifetime.

By exploring the many ways in which guide dogs improve the quality of life for their handlers, we gain a greater appreciation for the transformative power of these remarkable animals. Guide dogs are not just service animals; they are lifelines, partners, and friends who enable their handlers to live more fulfilling and independent lives.

CHAPTER TEN

The Future of Guide Dogs:

Innovations, Training, and Expanding

Accessibility

Introduction

The role of guide dogs in assisting individuals with visual impairments has been transformative for decades. From their origins as faithful companions and helpers to the sophisticated training programs they undergo today, guide dogs continue to improve the lives of people who are blind or have low vision. However, as technology advances and society continues to evolve, the future of guide dogs promises even greater innovations, improvements in training techniques, and expanded accessibility.

In this chapter, we will explore what the future holds for guide dogs, focusing on the role of technological innovations, advancements in training, and how we can expand accessibility to ensure that more individuals have access to the life-changing benefits of guide dog partnerships. Drawing on insights from experts in the field, as well as the latest trends and research, we will paint a picture of what the next generation of guide dog partnerships may look like.

1. Innovations in Technology and How They Integrate with Guide Dogs

1.1. Wearable Technology for Enhanced Mobility

As the world becomes increasingly tech-savvy, innovations in wearable technology are shaping how guide dogs and their handlers interact with their environment. New wearable devices designed specifically for individuals with visual impairments offer exciting possibilities for improving the mobility and safety of guide dog teams. These technologies are not meant to replace the essential role of guide dogs but to complement and enhance their guidance capabilities.

One such innovation is the use of smart glasses or headsets that offer real-time environmental feedback to the handler. These devices can detect objects, street signs, and even changes in terrain, providing auditory or haptic feedback to the handler. By combining this technology with the guide dog's guidance, handlers can experience a more comprehensive and dynamic sense of their surroundings.

Another example is the development of GPS-enabled wearables. These devices use advanced satellite navigation and mapping systems to provide precise location information, which can be relayed to both the handler and the guide dog. This integration allows for more efficient navigation in complex or unfamiliar environments, such as airports, shopping centers, and busy city streets. With the help of these technologies, handlers can gain additional layers of information that enhance their ability to make decisions and navigate safely.

In the future, it's conceivable that guide dogs and wearable technologies will work in synergy, enabling handlers to make even more informed choices about their routes and surroundings. These innovations will undoubtedly improve the quality of life for guide dog users, offering them more autonomy and confidence in their daily activities.

1.2. Smart Leashes and Collars

Another exciting area of innovation lies in the development of smart leashes and collars for guide dogs. These devices use sensors and connected technology to monitor the dog's movements and behaviors, providing valuable data that can help improve the dog's performance and well-being.

For example, a smart leash could track the dog's walking speed, direction, and distance traveled, offering real-time feedback to the handler about the dog's movements. This could be particularly useful for assessing the dog's training and ensuring that they are maintaining a consistent pace. Additionally, smart collars could monitor the dog's health metrics, such as heart rate, body temperature, and energy levels, ensuring that the dog remains healthy and comfortable throughout its workday.

These innovations in wearable technology will not only enhance the dog's performance but also provide handlers with greater insight into their guide dog's behavior and health. This data-driven approach will help to optimize the partnership between handler and guide dog, ensuring that both can continue to work together in the most effective and harmonious way possible.

2. Advancements in Guide Dog Training Methods

2.1. Positive Reinforcement and Cognitive Training

Guide dog training has come a long way since its early days, and today, trainers use a combination of advanced techniques and methods to ensure that the dogs are well-prepared to assist their handlers. One of the most significant developments in guide dog training is the widespread use of positive reinforcement. This training method focuses on rewarding desirable behaviors rather than punishing undesirable ones, which helps to foster a strong bond of trust and cooperation between the dog and its trainer.

Cognitive training techniques are also becoming more common in guide dog programs. These techniques are designed to stimulate the dog's problem-solving abilities and cognitive functions, enabling them to navigate complex environments more effectively. Dogs are taught to think critically about their surroundings and make decisions based on their handler's needs. For example, a dog might be trained to recognize when a handler is approaching a busy intersection and adjust its pace accordingly to ensure a safe crossing.

In the future, cognitive training will likely play an even greater role in guide dog programs, allowing dogs to adapt more quickly to new situations and handle increasingly complex environments. With the help of cognitive training, guide dogs will be able to learn new tasks and refine their skills more efficiently, ultimately providing better service to their handlers.

2.2. Personalized Training for Individual Needs

As more individuals with diverse visual impairments gain access to guide dogs, there is a growing need for personalized training programs that cater to the unique needs of each handler. While standard guide dog training has been effective for many years, personalized approaches are becoming increasingly important to ensure that each partnership is as successful as possible.

For example, some individuals may require guide dogs with specific skills or characteristics to address their particular needs. Handlers with additional mobility challenges, such as those who use a wheelchair, may require a guide dog that is particularly strong and skilled at navigating tight spaces. Similarly, individuals who are more familiar with certain environments, like rural areas, may need a guide dog that is specifically trained for outdoor navigation.

As we move into the future, personalized training will become more commonplace. Guide dog programs will increasingly focus on matching the right dog with the right handler based on their individual preferences, lifestyles, and abilities. This tailored approach will help ensure that both the dog and the handler can work together most effectively and comfortably.

2.3. Training for Urban and Technological Environments

In addition to personalized training, guide dogs will increasingly be trained to handle complex urban environments and technological spaces. The modern world is filled with distractions and hazards that were not present in earlier years, such as busy traffic, construction zones, and high-tech navigation tools. As cities become more crowded and technologically advanced, guide dogs will need to be trained to navigate these environments safely.

For example, guide dogs may need to learn to identify and avoid autonomous vehicles or navigate through crowded airports with advanced security systems. Additionally, the increasing prevalence of smart buildings and public spaces equipped with sensors and automated systems will require guide dogs to adapt to new forms of communication and guidance.

This type of specialized training will ensure that guide dogs remain valuable assets in the modern world, providing their handlers with the assistance they need in increasingly complex environments.

3. Expanding Accessibility and Inclusivity

3.1. Ensuring Equal Access to Guide Dogs

One of the primary challenges in the future of guide dogs is ensuring that individuals with visual impairments, regardless of their geographic location or socioeconomic status, have access to these life-changing animals. In many parts of the world, access to guide dogs remains limited, with long waiting lists for placements and a lack of available dogs.

Expanding access to guide dogs requires significant investments in training programs, breeding initiatives, and partnerships between guide dog organizations, governments, and communities. Collaborative efforts can help to ensure that more people around the world have the opportunity to receive a guide dog. Additionally, efforts should be made to reduce the financial barriers that often prevent individuals from obtaining guide dogs. Subsidies, grants, and sponsorships can help cover the costs of training and placement, making guide dogs more accessible to a wider range of individuals.

3.2. Promoting Public Awareness and Acceptance

In addition to expanding access to guide dogs, increasing public awareness and acceptance is essential. Many individuals with visual impairments face challenges when it comes to accessing public spaces or traveling on public transportation with their guide dogs. Public misconceptions about guide dogs and their role in society can create unnecessary barriers for handlers.

Education campaigns are crucial for promoting understanding and ensuring that guide dog users can move freely and confidently in public spaces. This includes informing the public about the rights of individuals with guide dogs, as well as the importance of respecting the partnership between handler and dog. As awareness grows, the social acceptance of guide dogs will continue to improve, leading to a more inclusive society.

3.3. International Collaboration and Standardization

As guide dog programs continue to grow worldwide, international collaboration and standardization will become increasingly important. Countries around the world have different regulations, training standards, and certifications for guide dogs, which can create barriers for individuals who wish to travel internationally or receive services from foreign guide dog organizations.

By collaborating on best practices and developing international standards for guide dog training, certification, and access, organizations can create a more unified and seamless experience for guide dog users across borders. This will help ensure that individuals with visual impairments can access guide dogs no matter where they are, promoting inclusivity and freedom of movement.

Conclusion

The future of guide dogs is filled with exciting possibilities. From advancements in wearable technology that enhance the guidance of dogs to innovations in personalized training, the partnership between guide dogs and their handlers is poised to evolve in remarkable ways. As we look ahead, it is essential that we continue to expand accessibility, promote inclusivity, and ensure that individuals with visual impairments have access to the life-changing benefits that guide dogs provide.

By embracing new technologies, refining training techniques, and fostering greater societal acceptance, we can ensure that the future of guide dogs remains bright, providing individuals with the mobility, independence, and confidence they need to thrive.

Refrences

Chapter 1: Introduction to Guide Dogs

- Guide Dogs for the Blind. (2023). About Guide Dogs. Guide Dogs for the Blind. https://www.guidedogs.com

- Hitt, L., & Blanchard, J. (2019). Guide dogs and their impact on independent living. The Journal of Visual Impairment & Blindness, 113(1), 10-18.

- Landers, P. (2018). The importance of guide dogs in the lives of visually impaired people. Journal of Disability and Rehabilitation, 40(1), 33-42.

Chapter 2: Understanding Visual Impairments and Mobility Needs

- World Health Organization (WHO). (2021). Visual impairment and blindness: A global overview. World Health Organization. https://www.who.int

- Perkins School for the Blind. (2020). Understanding vision loss. Perkins School for the Blind. https://www.perkins.org

- National Federation of the Blind. (2022). Living with vision loss. National Federation of the Blind. https://www.nfb.org

Chapter 3: Breeds Best Suited for Guide Dog Work

- Guide Dogs for the Blind. (2021). Best breeds for guide dogs. Guide Dogs for the Blind. https://www.guidedogs.com

- McNally, L. (2019). The best guide dog breeds: Characteristics and suitability. Journal of Service Animals and Training, 21(3), 45-56.

- National Guide Dogs Association. (2020). Choosing the right breed for guide dog work. National Guide Dog Association. https://www.ngda.org

Chapter 4: The Science of Breeding and Genetics in Guide Dogs

Andrews, C. (2020). Genetics and breeding in guide dogs: Ensuring success in service. Canine Genetics Journal, 19(4), 202-210.

Belanger, K. (2021). Breeding for performance: The science of guide dog genetics. Journal of Canine Genetics and Breeding, 23(2), 157-165.

Kall, D. (2022). Ethics and genetics in guide dog breeding. Ethics in Animal Breeding, 14(1), 88-95.

Chapter 5: Guide Dog Training: Techniques and Protocols

- Ralston, M. (2021). Training guide dogs: Methods for success. Dog Trainer's Guide, 18(5), 55-67.

- Falco, M. (2019). Positive reinforcement in guide dog training: A shift in paradigm. Training Dogs for Service. https://www.dogtrainers.com

- National Guide Dog School. (2020). Guide dog training process and key techniques. National Guide Dog School. https://www.ngds.org

Chapter 6: Challenges Faced in Guide Dog Training

- Walsh, J. (2021). Overcoming challenges in guide dog training: A comprehensive guide. Journal of Service Animals, 13(6), 23-37.

- Haines, S. (2022). Addressing behavioral issues in guide dog training. Canine Behavioral Science, 17(3), 145-154.

- Guide Dogs Australia. (2021). Training challenges and successes: A guide dog trainer's perspective. Guide Dogs Australia. https://www.guidedogs.com.au

Chapter 7: The Role of Guide Dogs in Mobility and Independence

- Gagne, M., & McGregor, P. (2020). The impact of guide dogs on mobility and independence. The Journal of Assistive Technology, 21(4), 58-66.

- Guide Dogs International. (2021). Guide dogs and independence: Life-changing partnerships. Guide Dogs International. https://www.guidedogsinternational.org

- Marshall, T. (2019). How guide dogs help people with visual impairments live more independently. The International Journal of Disability, 40(2), 200-208.

Chapter 8: The Lifelong Bond Between Guide Dog and Handler

- Kessler, T. (2022). The bond between guide dogs and their handlers: Building trust and partnership. Journal of Animal Behavior, 45(1), 88-101.

- McKinnon, J. (2021). Psychosocial benefits of having a guide dog: A review. Psychological Reports on Disability, 38(4), 102-115.

- Guide Dogs for the Blind. (2020). The bond between a guide dog and its handler. Guide Dogs for the Blind. https://www.guidedogs.com

Chapter 9: Innovations in Technology and Guide Dogs

- Pacifico, M. (2021). How GPS technology is enhancing guide dog use. Assistive Technology and Design. https://www.atalink.com

- Hernandez, M. (2020). Wearable technology and its impact on the visually impaired. Journal of Assistive Technology. https://www.journals.sagepub.com

- Wills, J. (2022). Cognitive approaches in guide dog training: Exploring new frontiers. Journal of Canine Behavior. https://www.caninejournal.com

Chapter 10: Future Directions for Guide Dog Services

- Brown, K., & Wilson, T. (2023). Expanding guide dog accessibility: Bridging gaps for those in need. Journal of Disability Studies. https://www.jds.org

- International Guide Dog Federation. (2023). Global standards for guide dog training and certification. IGDF. https://www.igdf.org.uk

- Weller, L. (2018). A brief history of guide dogs and their evolution. The Guide Dog Chronicles. https://www.guidedoghistory.com

WE VALUE YOUR FEEDBACK!

Thank you for reading Guide Dogs for the Blind: Training, Care, and Stories. I hope this book has provided you with valuable insights and inspiration about the incredible world of guide dogs.

If you found this book helpful, informative, or inspiring, I kindly ask you to take a moment to leave a review on Amazon. Your feedback not only helps other readers discover this book but also supports the mission of spreading awareness about guide dogs and their life-changing impact.

Your honest review makes a difference!

Leave a Review on Amazon

Thank you for your support!

Printed in Dunstable, United Kingdom